THIS BOOK BELONGS TO:

CONTACT INFORMATION	
NAME:	
ADDRESS:	
PHONE:	

START / END DATES

_____ / ___ / ___   TO   _____ / ___ / ___

Dedication

This Tea Tasting Journal is dedicated to all the tea tasting enthusiasts out there who want to record their tea tastings and document their findings in the process.

You are my inspiration for producing books and I'm honored to be a part of keeping all of your tea tasting notes and records organized.

This journal notebook will help you record the details of your tea tasting adventures.

Thoughtfully put together with these sections to record: Tea Name, Origin, Type, Brewing Method, Dry Leaves Amount, Water Temp, Steeping Time, Aroma, Liquor Taste, Aroma Checklist, and much more!

How to Use this Book

The purpose of this book is to keep all of your Tea Tasting notes all in one place. It will help keep you organized.

This Tea Tasting Notes Journal will allow you to accurately document every detail about your tea tasting adventures.

Here are examples of the prompts for you to fill in and write about your experience in this book:

1. Tea - Record the Name, Brand & Seller.
2. Origin - Write the country origin.
3. Type - Log whether it is Black, White, Green, Herbal, Oolong, Pu-erh, Fruit, or Other.
4. Brewing Method - Record details of the brewing method used.
5. Dry Leaves Amount - Write how many leaves were used.
6. Water Temp - Log the temperature.
7. Steeping Time - Record the amount of time it was steeped.
8. Aroma - Write anything you notice about the aroma.
9. Liquor Taste - Did you have any liquor taste?
10. Aroma Checklist - Check whether it was Bitter, Robust, Nutty, Spicy, Woodsy, Smokey, Earthy, Citrus, Flowery, Delicate, Sweet, Malty or Other.
11. Prepared With - Write whether you used Sugar, Cream, Milk, Lemon, Honey or Other
12. Where Purchased - Record where did you purchase the tea.
13. Notes - Blank lined space for journaling any important information such as, ideas, favorite flavors you want to remember, varieties you want tto try,
14. Would You Buy Again? - Check yes or no.
15. Rating - Log your rating from 1-5 stars.

tea tasting notes

date	tea (name/brand/seller)

country of orgin:	price

tea type

☐ black ☐ green ☐ white ☐ herbal ☐ oolong ☐ pu-erh ☐ fruit ☐ other _____

brewing method	dry leaves (amount)	water temp.	steeping time(s)

tea leaves	liquor (color)

aroma	liquor (taste)

aroma check list

☐ bitter ☐ robust ☐ nutty ☐ earthy ☐ citrus ☐ flowery ☐ sweet ☐ delicate ☐ malty

☐ spicy ☐ woodsy ☐ smokey ☐ other _____

prepared with

☐ sugar ☐ milk ☐ cream ☐ lemon ☐ honey ☐ other _____

notes

is this tea good iced?	where this tea was purchased
☐ yes ☐ no	

would you buy again?	ideal for	rating
☐ yes ☐ no		☆☆☆☆☆

tea tasting notes

date	tea (name/brand/seller)	
country of orgin:		price

tea type

☐ black ☐ green ☐ white ☐ herbal ☐ oolong ☐ pu-erh ☐ fruit ☐ other _____

brewing method	dry leaves (amount)	water temp.	steeping time(s)

tea leaves	liquor (color)

aroma	liquor (taste)

aroma check list

☐ bitter ☐ robust ☐ nutty ☐ earthy ☐ citrus ☐ flowery ☐ sweet ☐ delicate ☐ malty

☐ spciy ☐ woodsy ☐ smokey ☐ other _____

prepared with

☐ sugar ☐ milk ☐ cream ☐ lemon ☐ honey ☐ other _____

notes

is this tea good iced?	where this tea was purchased	
☐ yes ☐ no		
would you buy again?	ideal for	rating
☐ yes ☐ no		☆☆☆☆☆

tea tasting notes

date	tea (name/brand/seller)	
country of orgin:		price

tea type

☐ black ☐ green ☐ white ☐ herbal ☐ oolong ☐ pu-erh ☐ fruit ☐ other

brewing method	dry leaves (amount)	water temp.	steeping time(s)

tea leaves	liquor (color)
aroma	liquor (taste)

aroma check list

☐ bitter ☐ robust ☐ nutty ☐ earthy ☐ citrus ☐ flowery ☐ sweet ☐ delicate ☐ malty
☐ spciy ☐ woodsy ☐ smokey ☐ other

prepared with

☐ sugar ☐ milk ☐ cream ☐ lemon ☐ honey ☐ other

notes

is this tea good iced?	where this tea was purchased	
☐ yes ☐ no		
would you buy again?	ideal for	rating
☐ yes ☐ no		☆☆☆☆☆

tea tasting notes

date	tea (name/brand/seller)	
country of orgin:		price

tea type

☐ black ☐ green ☐ white ☐ herbal ☐ oolong ☐ puerh ☐ fruit ☐ other _____

brewing method	dry leaves (amount)	water temp.	steeping time(s)

tea leaves	liquor (color)
aroma	liquor (taste)

aroma check list

☐ bitter ☐ robust ☐ nutty ☐ earthy ☐ citrus ☐ flowery ☐ sweet ☐ delicate ☐ malty

☐ spicy ☐ woodsy ☐ smokey ☐ other _____

prepared with

☐ sugar ☐ milk ☐ cream ☐ lemon ☐ honey ☐ other _____

notes

is this tea good iced?	where this tea was purchased	
☐ yes ☐ no		
would you buy again?	ideal for	rating
☐ yes ☐ no		☆☆☆☆☆

tea tasting notes

date	tea (name/brand/seller)

country of orgin:	price

tea type

☐ black ☐ green ☐ white ☐ herbal ☐ oolong ☐ puerh ☐ fruit ☐ other _____

brewing method	dry leaves (amount)	water temp.	steeping time(s)

tea leaves	liquor (color)

aroma	liquor (taste)

aroma check list

☐ bitter ☐ robust ☐ nutty ☐ earthy ☐ citrus ☐ flowery ☐ sweet ☐ delicate ☐ malty

☐ spicy ☐ woodsy ☐ smokey ☐ other _____

prepared with

☐ sugar ☐ milk ☐ cream ☐ lemon ☐ honey ☐ other _____

notes

is this tea good iced?	where this tea was purchased	
☐ yes ☐ no		
would you buy again?	ideal for	rating
☐ yes ☐ no		☆☆☆☆☆

tea tasting notes

date	tea (name/brand/seller)

country of orgin:		price

tea type

☐ black ☐ green ☐ white ☐ herbal ☐ oolong ☐ puerh ☐ fruit ☐ other _____

brewing method	dry leaves (amount)	water temp.	steeping time(s)

tea leaves	liquor (color)

aroma	liquor (taste)

aroma check list

☐ bitter ☐ robust ☐ nutty ☐ earthy ☐ citrus ☐ flowery ☐ sweet ☐ delicate ☐ malty
☐ spicy ☐ woodsy ☐ smokey ☐ other _____

prepared with

☐ sugar ☐ milk ☐ cream ☐ lemon ☐ honey ☐ other _____

notes

is this tea good iced?	where this tea was purchased	
☐ yes ☐ no		

would you buy again?	ideal for	rating
☐ yes ☐ no		☆☆☆☆☆

tea tasting notes

date	tea (name/brand/seller)	
country of orgin:		price

tea type

☐ black ☐ green ☐ white ☐ herbal ☐ oolong ☐ pu-erh ☐ fruit ☐ other _____

brewing method	dry leaves (amount)	water temp.	steeping time(s)
tea leaves		liquor (color)	
aroma		liquor (taste)	

aroma check list

☐ bitter ☐ robust ☐ nutty ☐ earthy ☐ citrus ☐ flowery ☐ sweet ☐ delicate ☐ malty

☐ spciy ☐ woodsy ☐ smokey ☐ other _____

prepared with

☐ sugar ☐ milk ☐ cream ☐ lemon ☐ honey ☐ other _____

notes

is this tea good iced?	where this tea was purchased	
☐ yes ☐ no		
would you buy again?	ideal for	rating
☐ yes ☐ no		☆☆☆☆☆

tea tasting notes

date	tea (name/brand/seller)	
country of orgin:		price

tea type

☐ black   ☐ green   ☐ white   ☐ herbal   ☐ oolong   ☐ pu-erh   ☐ fruit   ☐ other _____

brewing method	dry leaves (amount)	water temp.	steeping time(s)

tea leaves	liquor (color)

aroma	liquor (taste)

aroma check list

☐ bitter   ☐ robust   ☐ nutty   ☐ earthy   ☐ citrus   ☐ flowery   ☐ sweet   ☐ delicate   ☐ malty

☐ spicy   ☐ woodsy   ☐ smokey   ☐ other _____

prepared with

☐ sugar   ☐ milk   ☐ cream   ☐ lemon   ☐ honey   ☐ other _____

notes

is this tea good iced?	where this tea was purchased	
☐ yes ☐ no		
would you buy again?	ideal for	rating
☐ yes ☐ no		☆☆☆☆☆

tea tasting notes

date	tea (name/brand/seller)	
country of orgin:		price

tea type

☐ black ☐ green ☐ white ☐ herbal ☐ oolong ☐ pu-erh ☐ fruit ☐ other

brewing method	dry leaves (amount)	water temp.	steeping time(s)

tea leaves	liquor (color)
aroma	liquor (taste)

aroma check list

☐ bitter ☐ robust ☐ nutty ☐ earthy ☐ citrus ☐ flowery ☐ sweet ☐ delicate ☐ malty

☐ spcy ☐ woodsy ☐ smokey ☐ other

prepared with

☐ sugar ☐ milk ☐ cream ☐ lemon ☐ honey ☐ other

notes

is this tea good iced?	where this tea was purchased	
☐ yes ☐ no		
would you buy again?	ideal for	rating
☐ yes ☐ no		☆☆☆☆☆

tea tasting notes

date	tea (name/brand/seller)	
country of orgin:		price

tea type

☐ black ☐ green ☐ white ☐ herbal ☐ oolong ☐ pu-erh ☐ fruit ☐ other _____

brewing method	dry leaves (amount)	water temp.	steeping time(s)

tea leaves	liquor (color)

aroma	liquor (taste)

aroma check list

☐ bitter ☐ robust ☐ nutty ☐ earthy ☐ citrus ☐ flowery ☐ sweet ☐ delicate ☐ malty

☐ spicy ☐ woodsy ☐ smokey ☐ other _____

prepared with

☐ sugar ☐ milk ☐ cream ☐ lemon ☐ honey ☐ other _____

notes

is this tea good iced?	where this tea was purchased	
☐ yes ☐ no		
would you buy again?	ideal for	rating
☐ yes ☐ no		☆ ☆ ☆ ☆ ☆

tea tasting notes

date	tea (name/brand/seller)	
country of orgin:		price

tea type

☐ black ☐ green ☐ white ☐ herbal ☐ oolong ☐ pu-erh ☐ fruit ☐ other _____

brewing method	dry leaves (amount)	water temp.	steeping time(s)

tea leaves	liquor (color)
aroma	liquor (taste)

aroma check list

☐ bitter ☐ robust ☐ nutty ☐ earthy ☐ citrus ☐ flowery ☐ sweet ☐ delicate ☐ malty
☐ spicy ☐ woodsy ☐ smokey ☐ other _____

prepared with

☐ sugar ☐ milk ☐ cream ☐ lemon ☐ honey ☐ other _____

notes

is this tea good iced? ☐ yes ☐ no	where this tea was purchased	
would you buy again? ☐ yes ☐ no	ideal for	rating ☆ ☆ ☆ ☆ ☆

tea tasting notes

date	tea (name/brand/seller)	
country of orgin:		price

tea type

☐ black ☐ green ☐ white ☐ herbal ☐ oolong ☐ pu-erh ☐ fruit ☐ other _____

brewing method	dry leaves (amount)	water temp.	steeping time(s)

tea leaves	liquor (color)

aroma	liquor (taste)

aroma check list

☐ bitter ☐ robust ☐ nutty ☐ earthy ☐ citrus ☐ flowery ☐ sweet ☐ delicate ☐ malty

☐ spicy ☐ woodsy ☐ smokey ☐ other _____

prepared with

☐ sugar ☐ milk ☐ cream ☐ lemon ☐ honey ☐ other _____

notes

is this tea good iced?	where this tea was purchased	
☐ yes ☐ no		
would you buy again?	ideal for	rating
☐ yes ☐ no		☆☆☆☆☆

tea tasting notes

date	tea (name/brand/seller)

country of orgin:	price

tea type

☐ black ☐ green ☐ white ☐ herbal ☐ oolong ☐ pu-erh ☐ fruit ☐ other _____

brewing method	dry leaves (amount)	water temp.	steeping time(s)

tea leaves	liquor (color)

aroma	liquor (taste)

aroma check list

☐ bitter ☐ robust ☐ nutty ☐ earthy ☐ citrus ☐ flowery ☐ sweet ☐ delicate ☐ malty

☐ spicy ☐ woodsy ☐ smokey ☐ other _____

prepared with

☐ sugar ☐ milk ☐ cream ☐ lemon ☐ honey ☐ other _____

notes

is this tea good iced?	where this tea was purchased
☐ yes ☐ no	

would you buy again?	ideal for	rating
☐ yes ☐ no		☆☆☆☆☆

tea tasting notes

date	tea (name/brand/seller)	
country of orgin:		price

tea type

☐ black ☐ green ☐ white ☐ herbal ☐ oolong ☐ pu-erh ☐ fruit ☐ other _____

brewing method	dry leaves (amount)	water temp.	steeping time(s)

tea leaves	liquor (color)

aroma	liquor (taste)

aroma check list

☐ bitter ☐ robust ☐ nutty ☐ earthy ☐ citrus ☐ flowery ☐ sweet ☐ delicate ☐ malty

☐ spciy ☐ woodsy ☐ smokey ☐ other _____

prepared with

☐ sugar ☐ milk ☐ cream ☐ lemon ☐ honey ☐ other _____

notes

is this tea good iced?	where this tea was purchased	
☐ yes ☐ no		
would you buy again?	ideal for	rating
☐ yes ☐ no		☆☆☆☆☆

tea tasting notes

date	tea (name/brand/seller)

country of origin:		price

tea type

☐ black ☐ green ☐ white ☐ herbal ☐ oolong ☐ pu-erh ☐ fruit ☐ other _____

brewing method	dry leaves (amount)	water temp.	steeping time(s)

tea leaves	liquor (color)

aroma	liquor (taste)

aroma check list

☐ bitter ☐ robust ☐ nutty ☐ earthy ☐ citrus ☐ flowery ☐ sweet ☐ delicate ☐ malty

☐ spicy ☐ woodsy ☐ smokey ☐ other _____

prepared with

☐ sugar ☐ milk ☐ cream ☐ lemon ☐ honey ☐ other _____

notes

is this tea good iced?	where this tea was purchased	
☐ yes ☐ no		
would you buy again?	ideal for	rating
☐ yes ☐ no		☆ ☆ ☆ ☆ ☆

tea tasting notes

date	tea (name/brand/seller)	
country of orgin:		price

tea type

☐ black ☐ green ☐ white ☐ herbal ☐ oolong ☐ pu-erh ☐ fruit ☐ other _____

brewing method	dry leaves (amount)	water temp.	steeping time(s)

tea leaves	liquor (color)

aroma	liquor (taste)

aroma check list

☐ bitter ☐ robust ☐ nutty ☐ earthy ☐ citrus ☐ flowery ☐ sweet ☐ delicate ☐ malty

☐ spicy ☐ woodsy ☐ smokey ☐ other _____

prepared with

☐ sugar ☐ milk ☐ cream ☐ lemon ☐ honey ☐ other _____

notes

is this tea good iced?	where this tea was purchased	
☐ yes ☐ no		
would you buy again?	ideal for	rating
☐ yes ☐ no		☆☆☆☆☆

tea tasting notes

date	tea (name/brand/seller)	
country of orgin:		price

tea type

☐ black ☐ green ☐ white ☐ herbal ☐ oolong ☐ pu-erh ☐ fruit ☐ other _____

brewing method	dry leaves (amount)	water temp.	steeping time(s)

tea leaves	liquor (color)

aroma	liquor (taste)

aroma check list

☐ bitter ☐ robust ☐ nutty ☐ earthy ☐ citrus ☐ flowery ☐ sweet ☐ delicate ☐ malty

☐ spicy ☐ woodsy ☐ smokey ☐ other _____

prepared with

☐ sugar ☐ milk ☐ cream ☐ lemon ☐ honey ☐ other _____

notes

is this tea good iced?	where this tea was purchased	
☐ yes ☐ no		
would you buy again?	ideal for	rating
☐ yes ☐ no		☆☆☆☆☆

tea tasting notes

date	tea (name/brand/seller)	
country of orgin:		price

tea type
☐ black ☐ green ☐ white ☐ herbal ☐ oolong ☐ pu-erh ☐ fruit ☐ other _____

brewing method	dry leaves (amount)	water temp.	steeping time(s)

tea leaves	liquor (color)

aroma	liquor (taste)

aroma check list
☐ bitter ☐ robust ☐ nutty ☐ earthy ☐ citrus ☐ flowery ☐ sweet ☐ delicate ☐ malty
☐ spicy ☐ woodsy ☐ smokey ☐ other _____

prepared with
☐ sugar ☐ milk ☐ cream ☐ lemon ☐ honey ☐ other _____

notes

is this tea good iced?	where this tea was purchased	
☐ yes ☐ no		
would you buy again?	ideal for	rating
☐ yes ☐ no		☆☆☆☆☆

tea tasting notes

date	tea (name/brand/seller)	
country of orgin:		price

tea type

☐ black ☐ green ☐ white ☐ herbal ☐ oolong ☐ pu-erh ☐ fruit ☐ other _____

brewing method	dry leaves (amount)	water temp.	steeping time(s)

tea leaves	liquor (color)
aroma	liquor (taste)

aroma check list

☐ bitter ☐ robust ☐ nutty ☐ earthy ☐ citrus ☐ flowery ☐ sweet ☐ delicate ☐ malty

☐ spicy ☐ woodsy ☐ smokey ☐ other _____

prepared with

☐ sugar ☐ milk ☐ cream ☐ lemon ☐ honey ☐ other _____

notes

is this tea good iced?	where this tea was purchased	
☐ yes ☐ no		
would you buy again?	ideal for	rating
☐ yes ☐ no		☆☆☆☆☆

tea tasting notes

date	tea (name/brand/seller)		
country of orgin:			price

tea type
☐ black ☐ green ☐ white ☐ herbal ☐ oolong ☐ pu-erh ☐ fruit ☐ other

brewing method	dry leaves (amount)	water temp.	steeping time(s)

tea leaves	liquor (color)
aroma	liquor (taste)

aroma check list
☐ bitter ☐ robust ☐ nutty ☐ earthy ☐ citrus ☐ flowery ☐ sweet ☐ delicate ☐ malty
☐ spciy ☐ woodsy ☐ smokey ☐ other

prepared with
☐ sugar ☐ milk ☐ cream ☐ lemon ☐ honey ☐ other

notes

is this tea good iced?	where this tea was purchased	
☐ yes ☐ no		
would you buy again?	ideal for	rating
☐ yes ☐ no		☆☆☆☆☆

tea tasting notes

date	tea (name/brand/seller)	
country of orgin:		price

tea type

☐ black ☐ green ☐ white ☐ herbal ☐ oolong ☐ pu-erh ☐ fruit ☐ other _____

brewing method	dry leaves (amount)	water temp.	steeping time(s)

tea leaves	liquor (color)

aroma	liquor (taste)

aroma check list

☐ bitter ☐ robust ☐ nutty ☐ earthy ☐ citrus ☐ flowery ☐ sweet ☐ delicate ☐ malty
☐ spciy ☐ woodsy ☐ smokey ☐ other _____

prepared with

☐ sugar ☐ milk ☐ cream ☐ lemon ☐ honey ☐ other _____

notes

is this tea good iced?	where this tea was purchased	
☐ yes ☐ no		
would you buy again?	ideal for	rating
☐ yes ☐ no		☆ ☆ ☆ ☆ ☆

tea tasting notes

date	tea (name/brand/seller)

country of orgin:		price

tea type

☐ black ☐ green ☐ white ☐ herbal ☐ oolong ☐ puerh ☐ fruit ☐ other _____

brewing method	dry leaves (amount)	water temp.	steeping time(s)

tea leaves	liquor (color)

aroma	liquor (taste)

aroma check list

☐ bitter ☐ robust ☐ nutty ☐ earthy ☐ citrus ☐ flowery ☐ sweet ☐ delicate ☐ malty

☐ spciy ☐ woodsy ☐ smokey ☐ other _____

prepared with

☐ sugar ☐ milk ☐ cream ☐ lemon ☐ honey ☐ other _____

notes

is this tea good iced?	where this tea was purchased	
☐ yes ☐ no		
would you buy again?	ideal for	rating
☐ yes ☐ no		☆☆☆☆☆

tea tasting notes

date	tea (name/brand/seller)

country of orgin:	price

tea type

☐ black ☐ green ☐ white ☐ herbal ☐ oolong ☐ pu-erh ☐ fruit ☐ other _____

brewing method	dry leaves (amount)	water temp.	steeping time(s)

tea leaves	liquor (color)

aroma	liquor (taste)

aroma check list

☐ bitter ☐ robust ☐ nutty ☐ earthy ☐ citrus ☐ flowery ☐ sweet ☐ delicate ☐ malty

☐ spicy ☐ woodsy ☐ smokey ☐ other _____

prepared with

☐ sugar ☐ milk ☐ cream ☐ lemon ☐ honey ☐ other _____

notes

is this tea good iced?	where this tea was purchased	
☐ yes ☐ no		
would you buy again?	ideal for	rating
☐ yes ☐ no		☆☆☆☆☆

tea tasting notes

date	tea (name/brand/seller)	
country of orgin:		price

tea type

☐ black ☐ green ☐ white ☐ herbal ☐ oolong ☐ pu-erh ☐ fruit ☐ other _____

brewing method	dry leaves (amount)	water temp.	steeping time(s)

tea leaves	liquor (color)

aroma	liquor (taste)

aroma check list

☐ bitter ☐ robust ☐ nutty ☐ earthy ☐ citrus ☐ flowery ☐ sweet ☐ delicate ☐ malty

☐ spciy ☐ woodsy ☐ smokey ☐ other _____

prepared with

☐ sugar ☐ milk ☐ cream ☐ lemon ☐ honey ☐ other _____

notes

is this tea good iced?	where this tea was purchased	
☐ yes ☐ no		
would you buy again?	ideal for	rating
☐ yes ☐ no		☆ ☆ ☆ ☆ ☆

tea tasting notes

date	tea (name/brand/seller)

country of orgin:	price

tea type

☐ black ☐ green ☐ white ☐ herbal ☐ oolong ☐ pu-erh ☐ fruit ☐ other

brewing method	dry leaves (amount)	water temp.	steeping time(s)

tea leaves	liquor (color)

aroma	liquor (taste)

aroma check list

☐ bitter ☐ robust ☐ nutty ☐ earthy ☐ citrus ☐ flowery ☐ sweet ☐ delicate ☐ malty

☐ spicy ☐ woodsy ☐ smokey ☐ other

prepared with

☐ sugar ☐ milk ☐ cream ☐ lemon ☐ honey ☐ other

notes

is this tea good iced?	where this tea was purchased	
☐ yes ☐ no		

would you buy again?	ideal for	rating
☐ yes ☐ no		☆☆☆☆☆

tea tasting notes

date	tea (name/brand/seller)	
country of orgin:		price

tea type

☐ black ☐ green ☐ white ☐ herbal ☐ oolong ☐ pu-erh ☐ fruit ☐ other

brewing method	dry leaves (amount)	water temp.	steeping time(s)

tea leaves	liquor (color)

aroma	liquor (taste)

aroma check list

☐ bitter ☐ robust ☐ nutty ☐ earthy ☐ citrus ☐ flowery ☐ sweet ☐ delicate ☐ malty

☐ spciy ☐ woodsy ☐ smokey ☐ other

prepared with

☐ sugar ☐ milk ☐ cream ☐ lemon ☐ honey ☐ other

notes

is this tea good iced?	where this tea was purchased	
☐ yes ☐ no		
would you buy again?	ideal for	rating
☐ yes ☐ no		☆☆☆☆☆

tea tasting notes

date	tea (name/brand/seller)	
country of origin:		price

tea type

☐ black ☐ green ☐ white ☐ herbal ☐ oolong ☐ pu-erh ☐ fruit ☐ other _____

brewing method	dry leaves (amount)	water temp.	steeping time(s)

tea leaves	liquor (color)

aroma	liquor (taste)

aroma check list

☐ bitter ☐ robust ☐ nutty ☐ earthy ☐ citrus ☐ flowery ☐ sweet ☐ delicate ☐ malty

☐ spicy ☐ woodsy ☐ smokey ☐ other _____

prepared with

☐ sugar ☐ milk ☐ cream ☐ lemon ☐ honey ☐ other _____

notes

is this tea good iced?	where this tea was purchased	
☐ yes ☐ no		
would you buy again?	ideal for	rating
☐ yes ☐ no		☆ ☆ ☆ ☆ ☆

tea tasting notes

date	tea (name/brand/seller)	
country of orgin:		price

tea type
☐ black ☐ green ☐ white ☐ herbal ☐ oolong ☐ pu-erh ☐ fruit ☐ other _____

brewing method	dry leaves (amount)	water temp.	steeping time(s)

tea leaves	liquor (color)
aroma	liquor (taste)

aroma check list

☐ bitter ☐ robust ☐ nutty ☐ earthy ☐ citrus ☐ flowery ☐ sweet ☐ delicate ☐ malty
☐ spicy ☐ woodsy ☐ smokey ☐ other _____

prepared with

☐ sugar ☐ milk ☐ cream ☐ lemon ☐ honey ☐ other _____

notes

is this tea good iced?	where this tea was purchased	
☐ yes ☐ no		
would you buy again?	ideal for	rating
☐ yes ☐ no		☆☆☆☆☆

tea tasting notes

date	tea (name/brand/seller)

country of origin:	price

tea type

☐ black   ☐ green   ☐ white   ☐ herbal   ☐ oolong   ☐ pu-erh   ☐ fruit   ☐ other _____

brewing method	dry leaves (amount)	water temp.	steeping time(s)

tea leaves	liquor (color)

aroma	liquor (taste)

aroma check list

☐ bitter   ☐ robust   ☐ nutty   ☐ earthy   ☐ citrus   ☐ flowery   ☐ sweet   ☐ delicate   ☐ malty

☐ spicy   ☐ woodsy   ☐ smokey   ☐ other _____

prepared with

☐ sugar   ☐ milk   ☐ cream   ☐ lemon   ☐ honey   ☐ other _____

notes

is this tea good iced?	where this tea was purchased
☐ yes ☐ no	

would you buy again?	ideal for	rating
☐ yes ☐ no		☆☆☆☆☆

tea tasting notes

date	tea (name/brand/seller)	
country of orgin:		price

tea type

☐ black ☐ green ☐ white ☐ herbal ☐ oolong ☐ pu-erh ☐ fruit ☐ other _____

brewing method	dry leaves (amount)	water temp.	steeping time(s)

tea leaves	liquor (color)
aroma	liquor (taste)

aroma check list

☐ bitter ☐ robust ☐ nutty ☐ earthy ☐ citrus ☐ flowery ☐ sweet ☐ delicate ☐ malty
☐ spcy ☐ woodsy ☐ smokey ☐ other _____

prepared with

☐ sugar ☐ milk ☐ cream ☐ lemon ☐ honey ☐ other _____

notes

is this tea good iced?	where this tea was purchased	
☐ yes ☐ no		
would you buy again?	ideal for	rating
☐ yes ☐ no		☆☆☆☆☆

tea tasting notes

date	tea (name/brand/seller)	
country of orgin:		price

tea type

☐ black ☐ green ☐ white ☐ herbal ☐ oolong ☐ pu-erh ☐ fruit ☐ other

brewing method	dry leaves (amount)	water temp.	steeping time(s)

tea leaves	liquor (color)

aroma	liquor (taste)

aroma check list

☐ bitter ☐ robust ☐ nutty ☐ earthy ☐ citrus ☐ flowery ☐ sweet ☐ delicate ☐ malty

☐ spicy ☐ woodsy ☐ smokey ☐ other

prepared with

☐ sugar ☐ milk ☐ cream ☐ lemon ☐ honey ☐ other

notes

is this tea good iced?	where this tea was purchased	
☐ yes ☐ no		
would you buy again?	ideal for	rating
☐ yes ☐ no		☆☆☆☆☆

tea tasting notes

date	tea (name/brand/seller)	
country of orgin:		price

tea type

☐ black ☐ green ☐ white ☐ herbal ☐ oolong ☐ pu-erh ☐ fruit ☐ other

brewing method	dry leaves (amount)	water temp.	steeping time(s)

tea leaves	liquor (color)

aroma	liquor (taste)

aroma check list

☐ bitter ☐ robust ☐ nutty ☐ earthy ☐ citrus ☐ flowery ☐ sweet ☐ delicate ☐ malty

☐ spciy ☐ woodsy ☐ smokey ☐ other _____

prepared with

☐ sugar ☐ milk ☐ cream ☐ lemon ☐ honey ☐ other _____

notes

is this tea good iced? ☐ yes ☐ no	where this tea was purchased	
would you buy again? ☐ yes ☐ no	ideal for	rating ☆☆☆☆☆

tea tasting notes

date	tea (name/brand/seller)

country of orgin:		price

tea type

☐ black ☐ green ☐ white ☐ herbal ☐ oolong ☐ pu-erh ☐ fruit ☐ other _____

brewing method	dry leaves (amount)	water temp.	steeping time(s)

tea leaves	liquor (color)

aroma	liquor (taste)

aroma check list

☐ bitter ☐ robust ☐ nutty ☐ earthy ☐ citrus ☐ flowery ☐ sweet ☐ delicate ☐ malty

☐ spicy ☐ woodsy ☐ smokey ☐ other _____

prepared with

☐ sugar ☐ milk ☐ cream ☐ lemon ☐ honey ☐ other _____

notes

is this tea good iced?	where this tea was purchased
☐ yes ☐ no	

would you buy again?	ideal for	rating
☐ yes ☐ no		☆ ☆ ☆ ☆ ☆

tea tasting notes

date	tea (name/brand/seller)	
country of orgin:		price
tea type ☐ black ☐ green ☐ white ☐ herbal ☐ oolong ☐ pu-erh ☐ fruit ☐ other		
brewing method	dry leaves (amount)	water temp.	steeping time(s)

tea leaves	liquor (color)
aroma	liquor (taste)

aroma check list

☐ bitter ☐ robust ☐ nutty ☐ earthy ☐ citrus ☐ flowery ☐ sweet ☐ delicate ☐ malty
☐ spciy ☐ woodsy ☐ smokey ☐ other

prepared with

☐ sugar ☐ milk ☐ cream ☐ lemon ☐ honey ☐ other

notes

is this tea good iced? ☐ yes ☐ no	where this tea was purchased	
would you buy again? ☐ yes ☐ no	ideal for	rating ☆☆☆☆☆

tea tasting notes

date	tea (name/brand/seller)

country of orgin:	price

tea type

☐ black ☐ green ☐ white ☐ herbal ☐ oolong ☐ pu-erh ☐ fruit ☐ other

brewing method	dry leaves (amount)	water temp.	steeping time(s)

tea leaves	liquor (color)

aroma	liquor (taste)

aroma check list

☐ bitter ☐ robust ☐ nutty ☐ earthy ☐ citrus ☐ flowery ☐ sweet ☐ delicate ☐ malty

☐ spicy ☐ woodsy ☐ smokey ☐ other _____

prepared with

☐ sugar ☐ milk ☐ cream ☐ lemon ☐ honey ☐ other _____

notes

is this tea good iced?	where this tea was purchased
☐ yes ☐ no	

would you buy again?	ideal for	rating
☐ yes ☐ no		☆☆☆☆☆

tea tasting notes

date	tea (name/brand/seller)	
country of orgin:		price

tea type

☐ black ☐ green ☐ white ☐ herbal ☐ oolong ☐ pu-erh ☐ fruit ☐ other _____

brewing method	dry leaves (amount)	water temp.	steeping time(s)

tea leaves	liquor (color)

aroma	liquor (taste)

aroma check list

☐ bitter ☐ robust ☐ nutty ☐ earthy ☐ citrus ☐ flowery ☐ sweet ☐ delicate ☐ malty

☐ spicy ☐ woodsy ☐ smokey ☐ other _____

prepared with

☐ sugar ☐ milk ☐ cream ☐ lemon ☐ honey ☐ other _____

notes

is this tea good iced?	where this tea was purchased	
☐ yes ☐ no		
would you buy again?	ideal for	rating
☐ yes ☐ no		☆☆☆☆☆

tea tasting notes

date	tea (name/brand/seller)

country of orgin:	price

tea type

☐ black ☐ green ☐ white ☐ herbal ☐ oolong ☐ pu-erh ☐ fruit ☐ other _____

brewing method	dry leaves (amount)	water temp.	steeping time(s)

tea leaves	liquor (color)

aroma	liquor (taste)

aroma check list

☐ bitter ☐ robust ☐ nutty ☐ earthy ☐ citrus ☐ flowery ☐ sweet ☐ delicate ☐ malty

☐ spicy ☐ woodsy ☐ smokey ☐ other _____

prepared with

☐ sugar ☐ milk ☐ cream ☐ lemon ☐ honey ☐ other _____

notes

is this tea good iced?	where this tea was purchased	
☐ yes ☐ no		
would you buy again?	ideal for	rating
☐ yes ☐ no		☆☆☆☆☆

tea tasting notes

date	tea (name/brand/seller)	
country of orgin:		price

tea type

☐ black ☐ green ☐ white ☐ herbal ☐ oolong ☐ pu-erh ☐ fruit ☐ other _____

brewing method	dry leaves (amount)	water temp.	steeping time(s)

tea leaves	liquor (color)
aroma	liquor (taste)

aroma check list

☐ bitter ☐ robust ☐ nutty ☐ earthy ☐ citrus ☐ flowery ☐ sweet ☐ delicate ☐ malty

☐ spciy ☐ woodsy ☐ smokey ☐ other _____

prepared with

☐ sugar ☐ milk ☐ cream ☐ lemon ☐ honey ☐ other _____

notes

is this tea good iced?	where this tea was purchased	
☐ yes ☐ no		
would you buy again?	ideal for	rating
☐ yes ☐ no		☆ ☆ ☆ ☆ ☆

tea tasting notes

date	tea (name/brand/seller)

country of orgin:	price

tea type

☐ black ☐ green ☐ white ☐ herbal ☐ oolong ☐ pu-erh ☐ fruit ☐ other _____

brewing method	dry leaves (amount)	water temp.	steeping time(s)

tea leaves	liquor (color)
aroma	liquor (taste)

aroma check list

☐ bitter ☐ robust ☐ nutty ☐ earthy ☐ citrus ☐ flowery ☐ sweet ☐ delicate ☐ malty

☐ spcy ☐ woodsy ☐ smokey ☐ other _____

prepared with

☐ sugar ☐ milk ☐ cream ☐ lemon ☐ honey ☐ other _____

notes

is this tea good iced?	where this tea was purchased
☐ yes ☐ no	
would you buy again?	**ideal for**	**rating**
☐ yes ☐ no		☆ ☆ ☆ ☆ ☆

tea tasting notes

date	tea (name/brand/seller)	
country of orgin:		price

tea type
☐ black ☐ green ☐ white ☐ herbal ☐ oolong ☐ pu-erh ☐ fruit ☐ other _____

brewing method	dry leaves (amount)	water temp.	steeping time(s)

tea leaves	liquor (color)

aroma	liquor (taste)

aroma check list
☐ bitter ☐ robust ☐ nutty ☐ earthy ☐ citrus ☐ flowery ☐ sweet ☐ delicate ☐ malty
☐ spicy ☐ woodsy ☐ smokey ☐ other _____

prepared with
☐ sugar ☐ milk ☐ cream ☐ lemon ☐ honey ☐ other _____

notes

is this tea good iced?	where this tea was purchased	
☐ yes ☐ no		
would you buy again?	ideal for	rating
☐ yes ☐ no		☆☆☆☆☆

tea tasting notes

date	tea (name/brand/seller)

country of orgin:	price

tea type

☐ black ☐ green ☐ white ☐ herbal ☐ oolong ☐ pu-erh ☐ fruit ☐ other _____

brewing method	dry leaves (amount)	water temp.	steeping time(s)

tea leaves	liquor (color)

aroma	liquor (taste)

aroma check list

☐ bitter ☐ robust ☐ nutty ☐ earthy ☐ citrus ☐ flowery ☐ sweet ☐ delicate ☐ malty

☐ spicy ☐ woodsy ☐ smokey ☐ other _____

prepared with

☐ sugar ☐ milk ☐ cream ☐ lemon ☐ honey ☐ other _____

notes

is this tea good iced?	where this tea was purchased
☐ yes ☐ no	

would you buy again?	ideal for	rating
☐ yes ☐ no		☆☆☆☆☆

tea tasting notes

date	tea (name/brand/seller)

country of orgin:		price

tea type

☐ black ☐ green ☐ white ☐ herbal ☐ oolong ☐ pu-erh ☐ fruit ☐ other _____

brewing method	dry leaves (amount)	water temp.	steeping time(s)

tea leaves	liquor (color)

aroma	liquor (taste)

aroma check list

☐ bitter ☐ robust ☐ nutty ☐ earthy ☐ citrus ☐ flowery ☐ sweet ☐ delicate ☐ malty

☐ spicy ☐ woodsy ☐ smokey ☐ other _____

prepared with

☐ sugar ☐ milk ☐ cream ☐ lemon ☐ honey ☐ other _____

notes

is this tea good iced?	where this tea was purchased	
☐ yes ☐ no		
would you buy again?	ideal for	rating
☐ yes ☐ no		☆☆☆☆☆

tea tasting notes

date	tea (name/brand/seller)		
country of orgin:			price
tea type ☐ black ☐ green ☐ white ☐ herbal ☐ oolong ☐ pu-erh ☐ fruit ☐ other _____			
brewing method	dry leaves (amount)	water temp.	steeping time(s)
tea leaves		liquor (color)	
aroma		liquor (taste)	
aroma check list ☐ bitter ☐ robust ☐ nutty ☐ earthy ☐ citrus ☐ flowery ☐ sweet ☐ delicate ☐ malty ☐ spicy ☐ woodsy ☐ smokey ☐ other _____			
prepared with ☐ sugar ☐ milk ☐ cream ☐ lemon ☐ honey ☐ other _____			
notes			
is this tea good iced? ☐ yes ☐ no	where this tea was purchased		
would you buy again? ☐ yes ☐ no	ideal for		rating ☆☆☆☆☆

tea tasting notes

date	tea (name/brand/seller)		
country of orgin:			price
tea type ☐ black ☐ green ☐ white ☐ herbal ☐ oolong ☐ pu-erh ☐ fruit ☐ other			
brewing method	dry leaves (amount)	water temp.	steeping time(s)

tea leaves	liquor (color)
aroma	liquor (taste)

aroma check list

☐ bitter ☐ robust ☐ nutty ☐ earthy ☐ citrus ☐ flowery ☐ sweet ☐ delicate ☐ malty
☐ spicy ☐ woodsy ☐ smokey ☐ other

prepared with

☐ sugar ☐ milk ☐ cream ☐ lemon ☐ honey ☐ other

notes

is this tea good iced? ☐ yes ☐ no	where this tea was purchased	
would you buy again? ☐ yes ☐ no	ideal for	rating ☆☆☆☆☆

tea tasting notes

date	tea (name/brand/seller)		
country of orgin:			price

tea type

☐ black ☐ green ☐ white ☐ herbal ☐ oolong ☐ pu-erh ☐ fruit ☐ other

brewing method	dry leaves (amount)	water temp.	steeping time(s)
tea leaves		liquor (color)	
aroma		liquor (taste)	

aroma check list

☐ bitter ☐ robust ☐ nutty ☐ earthy ☐ citrus ☐ flowery ☐ sweet ☐ delicate ☐ malty

☐ spicy ☐ woodsy ☐ smokey ☐ other

prepared with

☐ sugar ☐ milk ☐ cream ☐ lemon ☐ honey ☐ other

notes

is this tea good iced?	where this tea was purchased	
☐ yes ☐ no		
would you buy again?	ideal for	rating
☐ yes ☐ no		☆☆☆☆☆

tea tasting notes

date	tea (name/brand/seller)		
country of orgin:			price
tea type ☐ black ☐ green ☐ white ☐ herbal ☐ oolong ☐ puerh ☐ fruit ☐ other			
brewing method	dry leaves (amount)	water temp.	steeping time(s)
tea leaves		liquor (color)	
aroma		liquor (taste)	

aroma check list

☐ bitter ☐ robust ☐ nutty ☐ earthy ☐ citrus ☐ flowery ☐ sweet ☐ delicate ☐ nutty

☐ spicy ☐ woodsy ☐ smokey ☐ other

prepared with

☐ sugar ☐ milk ☐ cream ☐ lemon ☐ honey ☐ other

notes

is this tea good iced? ☐ yes ☐ no	where this tea was purchased	
would you buy again? ☐ yes ☐ no	ideal for	rating ☆☆☆☆☆

tea tasting notes

date	tea (name/brand/seller)

country of orgin:		price

tea type

☐ black ☐ green ☐ white ☐ herbal ☐ oolong ☐ pu-erh ☐ fruit ☐ other

brewing method	dry leaves (amount)	water temp.	steeping time(s)

tea leaves	liquor (color)
aroma	liquor (taste)

aroma check list

☐ bitter ☐ robust ☐ nutty ☐ earthy ☐ citrus ☐ flowery ☐ sweet ☐ delicate ☐ malty

☐ spciy ☐ woodsy ☐ smokey ☐ other

prepared with

☐ sugar ☐ milk ☐ cream ☐ lemon ☐ honey ☐ other

notes

is this tea good iced?	where this tea was purchased	
☐ yes ☐ no		
would you buy again?	ideal for	rating
☐ yes ☐ no		☆ ☆ ☆ ☆ ☆

tea tasting notes

date	tea (name/brand/seller)		
country of orgin:			price
tea type ☐ black ☐ green ☐ white ☐ herbal ☐ oolong ☐ pu-erh ☐ fruit ☐ other _____			
brewing method	dry leaves (amount)	water temp.	steeping time(s)
tea leaves		liquor (color)	
aroma		liquor (taste)	
aroma check list ☐ bitter ☐ robust ☐ nutty ☐ earthy ☐ citrus ☐ flowery ☐ sweet ☐ delicate ☐ malty ☐ spicy ☐ woodsy ☐ smokey ☐ other _____			
prepared with ☐ sugar ☐ milk ☐ cream ☐ lemon ☐ honey ☐ other _____			
notes			
is this tea good iced? ☐ yes ☐ no	where this tea was purchased		
would you buy again? ☐ yes ☐ no	ideal for		rating ☆☆☆☆☆

tea tasting notes

date	tea (name/brand/seller)

country of orgin:	price

tea type

☐ black ☐ green ☐ white ☐ herbal ☐ oolong ☐ puerh ☐ fruit ☐ other _____

brewing method	dry leaves (amount)	water temp.	steeping time(s)

tea leaves	liquor (color)

aroma	liquor (taste)

aroma check list

☐ bitter ☐ robust ☐ nutty ☐ earthy ☐ citrus ☐ flowery ☐ sweet ☐ delicate ☐ malty

☐ spicy ☐ woodsy ☐ smokey ☐ other _____

prepared with

☐ sugar ☐ milk ☐ cream ☐ lemon ☐ honey ☐ other _____

notes

is this tea good iced?	where this tea was purchased	
☐ yes ☐ no		

would you buy again?	ideal for	rating
☐ yes ☐ no		☆☆☆☆☆

tea tasting notes

date	tea (name/brand/seller)	
country of orgin:		price

tea type

☐ black ☐ green ☐ white ☐ herbal ☐ oolong ☐ pu-erh ☐ fruit ☐ other _____

brewing method	dry leaves (amount)	water temp.	steeping time(s)

tea leaves	liquor (color)

aroma	liquor (taste)

aroma check list

☐ bitter ☐ robust ☐ nutty ☐ earthy ☐ citrus ☐ flowery ☐ sweet ☐ delicate ☐ malty

☐ spicy ☐ woodsy ☐ smokey ☐ other _____

prepared with

☐ sugar ☐ milk ☐ cream ☐ lemon ☐ honey ☐ other _____

notes

is this tea good iced?	where this tea was purchased	
☐ yes ☐ no		
would you buy again?	ideal for	rating
☐ yes ☐ no		☆☆☆☆☆

tea tasting notes

date	tea (name/brand/seller)

country of orgin:	price

tea type

☐ black ☐ green ☐ white ☐ herbal ☐ oolong ☐ pu-erh ☐ fruit ☐ other _____

brewing method	dry leaves (amount)	water temp.	steeping time(s)

tea leaves	liquor (color)

aroma	liquor (taste)

aroma check list

☐ bitter ☐ robust ☐ nutty ☐ earthy ☐ citrus ☐ flowery ☐ sweet ☐ delicate ☐ malty

☐ spicy ☐ woodsy ☐ smokey ☐ other

prepared with

☐ sugar ☐ milk ☐ cream ☐ lemon ☐ honey ☐ other _____

notes

is this tea good iced?	where this tea was purchased	
☐ yes ☐ no		
would you buy again?	ideal for	rating
☐ yes ☐ no		☆☆☆☆☆

tea tasting notes

date	tea (name/brand/seller)

country of orgin:	price

tea type

☐ black ☐ green ☐ white ☐ herbal ☐ oolong ☐ pu-erh ☐ fruit ☐ other _____

brewing method	dry leaves (amount)	water temp.	steeping time(s)

tea leaves	liquor (color)

aroma	liquor (taste)

aroma check list

☐ bitter ☐ robust ☐ nutty ☐ earthy ☐ citrus ☐ flowery ☐ sweet ☐ delicate ☐ malty

☐ spicy ☐ woodsy ☐ smokey ☐ other _____

prepared with

☐ sugar ☐ milk ☐ cream ☐ lemon ☐ honey ☐ other _____

notes

is this tea good iced?	where this tea was purchased		
☐ yes ☐ no			
would you buy again?	ideal for	rating	☆☆☆☆☆
☐ yes ☐ no			

tea tasting notes

date	tea (name/brand/seller)	
country of orgin:		price

tea type

☐ black ☐ green ☐ white ☐ herbal ☐ oolong ☐ pu-erh ☐ fruit ☐ other _____

brewing method	dry leaves (amount)	water temp.	steeping time(s)

tea leaves	liquor (color)

aroma	liquor (taste)

aroma check list

☐ bitter ☐ robust ☐ nutty ☐ earthy ☐ citrus ☐ flowery ☐ sweet ☐ delicate ☐ malty

☐ spicy ☐ woodsy ☐ smokey ☐ other _____

prepared with

☐ sugar ☐ milk ☐ cream ☐ lemon ☐ honey ☐ other _____

notes

is this tea good iced?	where this tea was purchased	
☐ yes ☐ no		
would you buy again?	ideal for	rating
☐ yes ☐ no		☆☆☆☆☆

tea tasting notes

date	tea (name/brand/seller)

country of orgin:		price

tea type

☐ black ☐ green ☐ white ☐ herbal ☐ oolong ☐ pu-erh ☐ fruit ☐ other _____

brewing method	dry leaves (amount)	water temp.	steeping time(s)

tea leaves	liquor (color)

aroma	liquor (taste)

aroma check list

☐ bitter ☐ robust ☐ nutty ☐ earthy ☐ citrus ☐ flowery ☐ sweet ☐ delicate ☐ malty

☐ spcly ☐ woodsy ☐ smokey ☐ other _____

prepared with

☐ sugar ☐ milk ☐ cream ☐ lemon ☐ honey ☐ other _____

notes

is this tea good iced?	where this tea was purchased	
☐ yes ☐ no		
would you buy again?	ideal for	rating
☐ yes ☐ no		☆☆☆☆☆

tea tasting notes

date	tea (name/brand/seller)	
country of orgin:		price

tea type

☐ black ☐ green ☐ white ☐ herbal ☐ oolong ☐ pu-erh ☐ fruit ☐ other

brewing method	dry leaves (amount)	water temp.	steeping time(s)

tea leaves	liquor (color)

aroma	liquor (taste)

aroma check list

☐ bitter ☐ robust ☐ nutty ☐ earthy ☐ citrus ☐ flowery ☐ sweet ☐ delicate ☐ malty

☐ spicy ☐ woodsy ☐ smokey ☐ other

prepared with

☐ sugar ☐ milk ☐ cream ☐ lemon ☐ honey ☐ other

notes

is this tea good iced?	where this tea was purchased	
☐ yes ☐ no		
would you buy again?	ideal for	rating
☐ yes ☐ no		☆☆☆☆☆

tea tasting notes

date	tea (name/brand/seller)

country of orgin:		price

tea type

☐ black ☐ green ☐ white ☐ herbal ☐ oolong ☐ pu-erh ☐ fruit ☐ other _____

brewing method	dry leaves (amount)	water temp.	steeping time(s)

tea leaves	liquor (color)

aroma	liquor (taste)

aroma check list

☐ bitter ☐ robust ☐ nutty ☐ earthy ☐ citrus ☐ flowery ☐ sweet ☐ delicate ☐ malty

☐ spicy ☐ woodsy ☐ smokey ☐ other _____

prepared with

☐ sugar ☐ milk ☐ cream ☐ lemon ☐ honey ☐ other _____

notes

is this tea good iced?	where this tea was purchased	
☐ yes ☐ no		
would you buy again?	ideal for	rating
☐ yes ☐ no		☆☆☆☆☆

tea tasting notes

date	tea (name/brand/seller)

country of orgin:	price

tea type

☐ black ☐ green ☐ white ☐ herbal ☐ oolong ☐ pu-erh ☐ fruit ☐ other _____

brewing method	dry leaves (amount)	water temp.	steeping time(s)

tea leaves	liquor (color)

aroma	liquor (taste)

aroma check list

☐ bitter ☐ robust ☐ nutty ☐ earthy ☐ citrus ☐ flowery ☐ sweet ☐ delicate ☐ malty

☐ spciy ☐ woodsy ☐ smokey ☐ other _____

prepared with

☐ sugar ☐ milk ☐ cream ☐ lemon ☐ honey ☐ other _____

notes

is this tea good iced?	where this tea was purchased
☐ yes ☐ no	

would you buy again?	ideal for	rating
☐ yes ☐ no		☆ ☆ ☆ ☆ ☆

tea tasting notes

date	tea (name/brand/seller)	
country of orgin:		price

tea type

☐ black ☐ green ☐ white ☐ herbal ☐ oolong ☐ pu-erh ☐ fruit ☐ other _____

brewing method	dry leaves (amount)	water temp.	steeping time(s)

tea leaves	liquor (color)

aroma	liquor (taste)

aroma check list

☐ bitter ☐ robust ☐ nutty ☐ earthy ☐ citrus ☐ flowery ☐ sweet ☐ delicate ☐ malty
☐ spciy ☐ woodsy ☐ smokey ☐ other _____

prepared with

☐ sugar ☐ milk ☐ cream ☐ lemon ☐ honey ☐ other _____

notes

is this tea good iced?	where this tea was purchased	
☐ yes ☐ no		
would you buy again?	ideal for	rating
☐ yes ☐ no		☆☆☆☆☆

tea tasting notes

date	tea (name/brand/seller)	
country of orgin:		price

tea type

☐ black ☐ green ☐ white ☐ herbal ☐ oolong ☐ puerh ☐ fruit ☐ other _____

brewing method	dry leaves (amount)	water temp.	steeping time(s)

tea leaves	liquor (color)

aroma	liquor (taste)

aroma check list

☐ bitter ☐ robust ☐ nutty ☐ earthy ☐ citrus ☐ flowery ☐ sweet ☐ delicate ☐ malty

☐ spicy ☐ woodsy ☐ smokey ☐ other _____

prepared with

☐ sugar ☐ milk ☐ cream ☐ lemon ☐ honey ☐ other _____

notes

is this tea good iced?	where this tea was purchased
☐ yes ☐ no	
would you buy again?	ideal for	rating
☐ yes ☐ no		☆☆☆☆☆

tea tasting notes

date	tea (name/brand/seller)	
country of orgin:		price

tea type
☐ black ☐ green ☐ white ☐ herbal ☐ oolong ☐ pu-erh ☐ fruit ☐ other _____

brewing method	dry leaves (amount)	water temp.	steeping time(s)

tea leaves	liquor (color)

aroma	liquor (taste)

aroma check list
☐ bitter ☐ robust ☐ nutty ☐ earthy ☐ citrus ☐ flowery ☐ sweet ☐ delicate ☐ malty
☐ spicy ☐ woodsy ☐ smokey ☐ other _____

prepared with
☐ sugar ☐ milk ☐ cream ☐ lemon ☐ honey ☐ other _____

notes

is this tea good iced? ☐ yes ☐ no	where this tea was purchased	
would you buy again? ☐ yes ☐ no	ideal for	rating ☆☆☆☆☆

tea tasting notes

date	tea (name/brand/seller)

country of orgin:	price

tea type

☐ black   ☐ green   ☐ white   ☐ herbal   ☐ oolong   ☐ pu-erh   ☐ fruit   ☐ other

brewing method	dry leaves (amount)	water temp.	steeping time(s)

tea leaves	liquor (color)

aroma	liquor (taste)

aroma check list

☐ bitter   ☐ robust   ☐ nutty   ☐ earthy   ☐ citrus   ☐ flowery   ☐ sweet   ☐ delicate   ☐ malty

☐ spicy   ☐ woodsy   ☐ smokey   ☐ other

prepared with

☐ sugar   ☐ milk   ☐ cream   ☐ lemon   ☐ honey   ☐ other

notes

is this tea good iced?	where this tea was purchased
☐ yes ☐ no	

would you buy again?	ideal for	rating
☐ yes ☐ no		☆☆☆☆☆

tea tasting notes

date	tea (name/brand/seller)	
country of orgin:		price

tea type

☐ black ☐ green ☐ white ☐ herbal ☐ oolong ☐ pu-erh ☐ fruit ☐ other

brewing method	dry leaves (amount)	water temp.	steeping time(s)

tea leaves	liquor (color)

aroma	liquor (taste)

aroma check list

☐ bitter ☐ robust ☐ nutty ☐ earthy ☐ citrus ☐ flowery ☐ sweet ☐ delicate ☐ malty

☐ spcy ☐ woodsy ☐ smokey ☐ other _____

prepared with

☐ sugar ☐ milk ☐ cream ☐ lemon ☐ honey ☐ other _____

notes

is this tea good iced?	where this tea was purchased	
☐ yes ☐ no		
would you buy again?	ideal for	rating
☐ yes ☐ no		☆☆☆☆☆

tea tasting notes

date	tea (name/brand/seller)

country of orgin:	price

tea type

☐ black ☐ green ☐ white ☐ herbal ☐ oolong ☐ pu-erh ☐ fruit ☐ other _____

brewing method	dry leaves (amount)	water temp.	steeping time(s)

tea leaves	liquor (color)

aroma	liquor (taste)

aroma check list

☐ bitter ☐ robust ☐ nutty ☐ earthy ☐ citrus ☐ flowery ☐ sweet ☐ delicate ☐ malty

☐ spicy ☐ woodsy ☐ smokey ☐ other _____

prepared with

☐ sugar ☐ milk ☐ cream ☐ lemon ☐ honey ☐ other _____

notes

is this tea good iced?	where this tea was purchased
☐ yes ☐ no	

would you buy again?	ideal for	rating
☐ yes ☐ no		☆☆☆☆☆

tea tasting notes

date	tea (name/brand/seller)	
country of orgin:		price

tea type

☐ black ☐ green ☐ white ☐ herbal ☐ oolong ☐ puerh ☐ fruit ☐ other _____

brewing method	dry leaves (amount)	water temp.	steeping time(s)

tea leaves	liquor (color)

aroma	liquor (taste)

aroma check list

☐ bitter ☐ robust ☐ nutty ☐ earthy ☐ citrus ☐ flowery ☐ sweet ☐ delicate ☐ malty

☐ spicy ☐ woodsy ☐ smokey ☐ other _____

prepared with

☐ sugar ☐ milk ☐ cream ☐ lemon ☐ honey ☐ other _____

notes

is this tea good iced?	where this tea was purchased	
☐ yes ☐ no		
would you buy again?	ideal for	rating
☐ yes ☐ no		☆☆☆☆☆

tea tasting notes

date	tea (name/brand/seller)

country of orgin:		price

tea type

☐ black ☐ green ☐ white ☐ herbal ☐ oolong ☐ pu-erh ☐ fruit ☐ other _____

brewing method	dry leaves (amount)	water temp.	steeping time(s)

tea leaves	liquor (color)

aroma	liquor (taste)

aroma check list

☐ bitter ☐ robust ☐ nutty ☐ earthy ☐ citrus ☐ flowery ☐ sweet ☐ delicate ☐ malty

☐ spicy ☐ woodsy ☐ smokey ☐ other _____

prepared with

☐ sugar ☐ milk ☐ cream ☐ lemon ☐ honey ☐ other _____

notes

is this tea good iced?	where this tea was purchased	
☐ yes ☐ no		

would you buy again?	ideal for	rating
☐ yes ☐ no		☆☆☆☆☆

tea tasting notes

date	tea (name/brand/seller)

country of orgin:		price

tea type

☐ black ☐ green ☐ white ☐ herbal ☐ oolong ☐ puerh ☐ fruit ☐ other _____

brewing method	dry leaves (amount)	water temp.	steeping time(s)

tea leaves	liquor (color)

aroma	liquor (taste)

aroma check list

☐ bitter ☐ robust ☐ nutty ☐ earthy ☐ citrus ☐ flowery ☐ sweet ☐ delicate ☐ malty

☐ spicy ☐ woodsy ☐ smokey ☐ other _____

prepared with

☐ sugar ☐ milk ☐ cream ☐ lemon ☐ honey ☐ other _____

notes

is this tea good iced?	where this tea was purchased	
☐ yes ☐ no		
would you buy again?	ideal for	rating
☐ yes ☐ no		☆ ☆ ☆ ☆ ☆

tea tasting notes

date	tea (name/brand/seller)

country of orgin:	price

tea type

☐ black ☐ green ☐ white ☐ herbal ☐ oolong ☐ pu-erh ☐ fruit ☐ other _____

brewing method	dry leaves (amount)	water temp.	steeping time(s)

tea leaves	liquor (color)
aroma	liquor (taste)

aroma check list

☐ bitter ☐ robust ☐ nutty ☐ earthy ☐ citrus ☐ flowery ☐ sweet ☐ delicate ☐ malty

☐ spicy ☐ woodsy ☐ smokey ☐ other _____

prepared with

☐ sugar ☐ milk ☐ cream ☐ lemon ☐ honey ☐ other _____

notes

is this tea good iced?	where this tea was purchased
☐ yes ☐ no	
would you buy again?	ideal for	rating
☐ yes ☐ no		☆☆☆☆☆

tea tasting notes

date	tea (name/brand/seller)	
country of orgin:		price

tea type

☐ black ☐ green ☐ white ☐ herbal ☐ oolong ☐ pu-erh ☐ fruit ☐ other _____

brewing method	dry leaves (amount)	water temp.	steeping time(s)

tea leaves	liquor (color)

aroma	liquor (taste)

aroma check list

☐ bitter ☐ robust ☐ nutty ☐ earthy ☐ citrus ☐ flowery ☐ sweet ☐ delicate ☐ malty

☐ spicy ☐ woodsy ☐ smokey ☐ other _____

prepared with

☐ sugar ☐ milk ☐ cream ☐ lemon ☐ honey ☐ other _____

notes

is this tea good iced?	where this tea was purchased	
☐ yes ☐ no		
would you buy again?	ideal for	rating
☐ yes ☐ no		☆☆☆☆☆

tea tasting notes

date	tea (name/brand/seller)

country of orgin:		price

tea type

☐ black   ☐ green   ☐ white   ☐ herbal   ☐ oolong   ☐ pu-erh   ☐ fruit   ☐ other _____

brewing method	dry leaves (amount)	water temp.	steeping time(s)

tea leaves	liquor (color)

aroma	liquor (taste)

aroma check list

☐ bitter   ☐ robust   ☐ nutty   ☐ earthy   ☐ citrus   ☐ flowery   ☐ sweet   ☐ delicate   ☐ malty

☐ spicy   ☐ woodsy   ☐ smokey   ☐ other _____

prepared with

☐ sugar   ☐ milk   ☐ cream   ☐ lemon   ☐ honey   ☐ other _____

notes

is this tea good iced?	where this tea was purchased	
☐ yes ☐ no		
would you buy again?	ideal for	rating
☐ yes ☐ no		☆ ☆ ☆ ☆ ☆

tea tasting notes

date	tea (name/brand/seller)

country of orgin:		price

tea type

☐ black ☐ green ☐ white ☐ herbal ☐ oolong ☐ pu-erh ☐ fruit ☐ other _____

brewing method	dry leaves (amount)	water temp.	steeping time(s)

tea leaves	liquor (color)

aroma	liquor (taste)

aroma check list

☐ bitter ☐ robust ☐ nutty ☐ earthy ☐ citrus ☐ flowery ☐ sweet ☐ delicate ☐ malty

☐ spicy ☐ woodsy ☐ smokey ☐ other _____

prepared with

☐ sugar ☐ milk ☐ cream ☐ lemon ☐ honey ☐ other _____

notes

is this tea good iced?	where this tea was purchased	
☐ yes ☐ no		
would you buy again?	ideal for	rating
☐ yes ☐ no		☆☆☆☆☆

tea tasting notes

date	tea (name/brand/seller)

country of orgin:	price

tea type

☐ black ☐ green ☐ white ☐ herbal ☐ oolong ☐ pu-erh ☐ fruit ☐ other _____

brewing method	dry leaves (amount)	water temp.	steeping time(s)

tea leaves	liquor (color)

aroma	liquor (taste)

aroma check list

☐ bitter ☐ robust ☐ nutty ☐ earthy ☐ citrus ☐ flowery ☐ sweet ☐ delicate ☐ malty

☐ spicy ☐ woodsy ☐ smokey ☐ other _____

prepared with

☐ sugar ☐ milk ☐ cream ☐ lemon ☐ honey ☐ other _____

notes

is this tea good iced?	where this tea was purchased
☐ yes ☐ no	

would you buy again?	ideal for	rating
☐ yes ☐ no		☆☆☆☆☆

tea tasting notes

date	tea (name/brand/seller)

country of orgin:		price

tea type

☐ black ☐ green ☐ white ☐ herbal ☐ oolong ☐ pu-erh ☐ fruit ☐ other _____

brewing method	dry leaves (amount)	water temp.	steeping time(s)

tea leaves	liquor (color)

aroma	liquor (taste)

aroma check list

☐ bitter ☐ robust ☐ nutty ☐ earthy ☐ citrus ☐ flowery ☐ sweet ☐ delicate ☐ malty

☐ spicy ☐ woodsy ☐ smokey ☐ other _____

prepared with

☐ sugar ☐ milk ☐ cream ☐ lemon ☐ honey ☐ other _____

notes

is this tea good iced?	where this tea was purchased	
☐ yes ☐ no		
would you buy again?	ideal for	rating
☐ yes ☐ no		☆ ☆ ☆ ☆ ☆

tea tasting notes

date	tea (name/brand/seller)

country of orgin:		price

tea type

☐ black ☐ green ☐ white ☐ herbal ☐ oolong ☐ pu-erh ☐ fruit ☐ other _____

brewing method	dry leaves (amount)	water temp.	steeping time(s)

tea leaves	liquor (color)
aroma	liquor (taste)

aroma check list

☐ bitter ☐ robust ☐ nutty ☐ earthy ☐ citrus ☐ flowery ☐ sweet ☐ delicate ☐ malty

☐ spicy ☐ woodsy ☐ smokey ☐ other _____

prepared with

☐ sugar ☐ milk ☐ cream ☐ lemon ☐ honey ☐ other _____

notes

is this tea good iced?	where this tea was purchased	
☐ yes ☐ no		
would you buy again?	ideal for	rating
☐ yes ☐ no		☆☆☆☆☆

tea tasting notes

date	tea (name/brand/seller)

country of orgin:		price

tea type

☐ black ☐ green ☐ white ☐ herbal ☐ oolong ☐ pu-erh ☐ fruit ☐ other _____

brewing method	dry leaves (amount)	water temp.	steeping time(s)

tea leaves	liquor (color)

aroma	liquor (taste)

aroma check list

☐ bitter ☐ robust ☐ nutty ☐ earthy ☐ citrus ☐ flowery ☐ sweet ☐ delicate ☐ malty

☐ spicy ☐ woodsy ☐ smokey ☐ other _____

prepared with

☐ sugar ☐ milk ☐ cream ☐ lemon ☐ honey ☐ other _____

notes

is this tea good iced?	where this tea was purchased	
☐ yes ☐ no		

would you buy again?	ideal for	rating
☐ yes ☐ no		☆☆☆☆☆

tea tasting notes

date	tea (name/brand/seller)

country of orgin:	price

tea type

☐ black ☐ green ☐ white ☐ herbal ☐ oolong ☐ pu-erh ☐ fruit ☐ other _____

brewing method	dry leaves (amount)	water temp.	steeping time(s)

tea leaves	liquor (color)

aroma	liquor (taste)

aroma check list

☐ bitter ☐ robust ☐ nutty ☐ earthy ☐ citrus ☐ flowery ☐ sweet ☐ delicate ☐ malty

☐ spciy ☐ woodsy ☐ smokey ☐ other _____

prepared with

☐ sugar ☐ milk ☐ cream ☐ lemon ☐ honey ☐ other _____

notes

is this tea good iced?	where this tea was purchased
☐ yes ☐ no	

would you buy again?	ideal for	rating
☐ yes ☐ no		☆☆☆☆☆

tea tasting notes

date	tea (name/brand/seller)		
country of orgin:			price

tea type

☐ black ☐ green ☐ white ☐ herbal ☐ oolong ☐ puerh ☐ fruit ☐ other _____

brewing method	dry leaves (amount)	water temp.	steeping time(s)

tea leaves	liquor (color)
aroma	liquor (taste)

aroma check list

☐ bitter ☐ robust ☐ nutty ☐ earthy ☐ citrus ☐ flowery ☐ sweet ☐ delicate ☐ malty

☐ spcy ☐ woodsy ☐ smokey ☐ other _____

prepared with

☐ sugar ☐ milk ☐ cream ☐ lemon ☐ honey ☐ other _____

notes

is this tea good iced?	where this tea was purchased	
☐ yes ☐ no		
would you buy again?	ideal for	rating
☐ yes ☐ no		☆☆☆☆☆

tea tasting notes

date	tea (name/brand/seller)	
country of orgin:		price

tea type

☐ black ☐ green ☐ white ☐ herbal ☐ oolong ☐ pu-erh ☐ fruit ☐ other _____

brewing method	dry leaves (amount)	water temp.	steeping time(s)

tea leaves	liquor (color)
aroma	liquor (taste)

aroma check list

☐ bitter ☐ robust ☐ nutty ☐ earthy ☐ citrus ☐ flowery ☐ sweet ☐ delicate ☐ malty

☐ spciy ☐ woodsy ☐ smokey ☐ other _____

prepared with

☐ sugar ☐ milk ☐ cream ☐ lemon ☐ honey ☐ other _____

notes

is this tea good iced? ☐ yes ☐ no	where this tea was purchased	
would you buy again? ☐ yes ☐ no	ideal for	rating ☆☆☆☆☆

tea tasting notes

date	tea (name/brand/seller)	
country of orgin:		price

tea type

☐ black   ☐ green   ☐ white   ☐ herbal   ☐ oolong   ☐ pu-erh   ☐ fruit   ☐ other _____

brewing method	dry leaves (amount)	water temp.	steeping time(s)
tea leaves		liquor (color)	
aroma		liquor (taste)	

aroma check list

☐ bitter   ☐ robust   ☐ nutty   ☐ earthy   ☐ citrus   ☐ flowery   ☐ sweet   ☐ delicate   ☐ malty

☐ spciy   ☐ woodsy   ☐ smokey   ☐ other _____

prepared with

☐ sugar   ☐ milk   ☐ cream   ☐ lemon   ☐ honey   ☐ other _____

notes

is this tea good iced?	where this tea was purchased	
☐ yes ☐ no		
would you buy again?	ideal for	rating
☐ yes ☐ no		☆ ☆ ☆ ☆ ☆

tea tasting notes

date	tea (name/brand/seller)

country of orgin:	price

tea type

☐ black   ☐ green   ☐ white   ☐ herbal   ☐ oolong   ☐ puerh   ☐ fruit   ☐ other _____

brewing method	dry leaves (amount)	water temp.	steeping time(s)

tea leaves	liquor (color)

aroma	liquor (taste)

aroma check list

☐ bitter   ☐ robust   ☐ nutty   ☐ earthy   ☐ citrus   ☐ flowery   ☐ sweet   ☐ delicate   ☐ malty

☐ spicy   ☐ woodsy   ☐ smokey   ☐ other _____

prepared with

☐ sugar   ☐ milk   ☐ cream   ☐ lemon   ☐ honey   ☐ other _____

notes

is this tea good iced?	where this tea was purchased
☐ yes ☐ no	

would you buy again?	ideal for	rating
☐ yes ☐ no		☆☆☆☆☆

tea tasting notes

date	tea (name/brand/seller)	
country of orgin:		price

tea type

☐ black ☐ green ☐ white ☐ herbal ☐ oolong ☐ pu-erh ☐ fruit ☐ other _____

brewing method	dry leaves (amount)	water temp.	steeping time(s)

tea leaves	liquor (color)

aroma	liquor (taste)

aroma check list

☐ bitter ☐ robust ☐ nutty ☐ earthy ☐ citrus ☐ flowery ☐ sweet ☐ delicate ☐ malty

☐ spcly ☐ woodsy ☐ smokey ☐ other _____

prepared with

☐ sugar ☐ milk ☐ cream ☐ lemon ☐ honey ☐ other _____

notes

is this tea good iced?	where this tea was purchased	
☐ yes ☐ no		
would you buy again?	ideal for	rating
☐ yes ☐ no		☆☆☆☆☆

tea tasting notes

date	tea (name/brand/seller)

country of orgin:	price

tea type

☐ black   ☐ green   ☐ white   ☐ herbal   ☐ oolong   ☐ pu-erh   ☐ fruit   ☐ other _____

brewing method	dry leaves (amount)	water temp.	steeping time(s)

tea leaves	liquor (color)

aroma	liquor (taste)

aroma check list

☐ bitter   ☐ robust   ☐ nutty   ☐ earthy   ☐ citrus   ☐ flowery   ☐ sweet   ☐ delicate   ☐ malty

☐ spciy   ☐ woodsy   ☐ smokey   ☐ other _____

prepared with

☐ sugar   ☐ milk   ☐ cream   ☐ lemon   ☐ honey   ☐ other _____

notes

is this tea good iced?	where this tea was purchased
☐ yes ☐ no	

would you buy again?	ideal for	rating
☐ yes ☐ no		☆ ☆ ☆ ☆ ☆

tea tasting notes

date	tea (name/brand/seller)

country of orgin:		price

tea type

☐ black ☐ green ☐ white ☐ herbal ☐ oolong ☐ puerh ☐ fruit ☐ other _____

brewing method	dry leaves (amount)	water temp.	steeping time(s)

tea leaves	liquor (color)

aroma	liquor (taste)

aroma check list

☐ bitter ☐ robust ☐ nutty ☐ earthy ☐ citrus ☐ flowery ☐ sweet ☐ delicate ☐ malty

☐ spicy ☐ woodsy ☐ smokey ☐ other _____

prepared with

☐ sugar ☐ milk ☐ cream ☐ lemon ☐ honey ☐ other _____

notes

is this tea good iced?	where this tea was purchased	
☐ yes ☐ no		
would you buy again?	ideal for	rating
☐ yes ☐ no		☆☆☆☆☆

tea tasting notes

date	tea (name/brand/seller)

country of orgin:		price

tea type

☐ black ☐ green ☐ white ☐ herbal ☐ oolong ☐ puerh ☐ fruit ☐ other _____

brewing method	dry leaves (amount)	water temp.	steeping time(s)

tea leaves	liquor (color)

aroma	liquor (taste)

aroma check list

☐ bitter ☐ robust ☐ nutty ☐ earthy ☐ citrus ☐ flowery ☐ sweet ☐ delicate ☐ malty

☐ spicy ☐ woodsy ☐ smokey ☐ other _____

prepared with

☐ sugar ☐ milk ☐ cream ☐ lemon ☐ honey ☐ other _____

notes

is this tea good iced?	where this tea was purchased	
☐ yes ☐ no		
would you buy again?	ideal for	rating
☐ yes ☐ no		☆☆☆☆☆

tea tasting notes

date	tea (name/brand/seller)	
country of orgin:		price

tea type

☐ black ☐ green ☐ white ☐ herbal ☐ oolong ☐ pu-erh ☐ fruit ☐ other _____

brewing method	dry leaves (amount)	water temp.	steeping time(s)

tea leaves	liquor (color)
aroma	liquor (taste)

aroma check list

☐ bitter ☐ robust ☐ nutty ☐ earthy ☐ citrus ☐ flowery ☐ sweet ☐ delicate ☐ malty

☐ spciy ☐ woodsy ☐ smokey ☐ other _____

prepared with

☐ sugar ☐ milk ☐ cream ☐ lemon ☐ honey ☐ other _____

notes

is this tea good iced? ☐ yes ☐ no	where this tea was purchased	
would you buy again? ☐ yes ☐ no	ideal for	rating ☆ ☆ ☆ ☆ ☆

tea tasting notes

date	tea (name/brand/seller)

country of orgin:	price

tea type

☐ black ☐ green ☐ white ☐ herbal ☐ oolong ☐ puerh ☐ fruit ☐ other _____

brewing method	dry leaves (amount)	water temp.	steeping time(s)

tea leaves	liquor (color)

aroma	liquor (taste)

aroma check list

☐ bitter ☐ robust ☐ nutty ☐ earthy ☐ citrus ☐ flowery ☐ sweet ☐ delicate ☐ malty

☐ spicy ☐ woodsy ☐ smokey ☐ other _____

prepared with

☐ sugar ☐ milk ☐ cream ☐ lemon ☐ honey ☐ other _____

notes

is this tea good iced?	where this tea was purchased
☐ yes ☐ no	

would you buy again?	ideal for	rating
☐ yes ☐ no		☆☆☆☆☆

tea tasting notes

date	tea (name/brand/seller)	
country of orgin:		price

tea type

☐ black ☐ green ☐ white ☐ herbal ☐ oolong ☐ puerh ☐ fruit ☐ other _____

brewing method	dry leaves (amount)	water temp.	steeping time(s)

tea leaves	liquor (color)
aroma	liquor (taste)

aroma check list

☐ bitter ☐ robust ☐ nutty ☐ earthy ☐ citrus ☐ flowery ☐ sweet ☐ delicate ☐ malty

☐ spciy ☐ woodsy ☐ smokey ☐ other _____

prepared with

☐ sugar ☐ milk ☐ cream ☐ lemon ☐ honey ☐ other _____

notes

is this tea good iced? ☐ yes ☐ no	where this tea was purchased	
would you buy again? ☐ yes ☐ no	ideal for	rating ☆☆☆☆☆

tea tasting notes

date	tea (name/brand/seller)	
country of orgin:		price

tea type

☐ black ☐ green ☐ white ☐ herbal ☐ oolong ☐ pu-erh ☐ fruit ☐ other _____

brewing method	dry leaves (amount)	water temp.	steeping time(s)

tea leaves	liquor (color)

aroma	liquor (taste)

aroma check list

☐ bitter ☐ robust ☐ nutty ☐ earthy ☐ citrus ☐ flowery ☐ sweet ☐ delicate ☐ malty
☐ spicy ☐ woodsy ☐ smokey ☐ other _____

prepared with

☐ sugar ☐ milk ☐ cream ☐ lemon ☐ honey ☐ other _____

notes

is this tea good iced? ☐ yes ☐ no	where this tea was purchased	
would you buy again? ☐ yes ☐ no	ideal for	rating ☆☆☆☆☆

tea tasting notes

date	tea (name/brand/seller)

country of orgin:		price

tea type

☐ black ☐ green ☐ white ☐ herbal ☐ oolong ☐ pu-erh ☐ fruit ☐ other _____

brewing method	dry leaves (amount)	water temp.	steeping time(s)

tea leaves	liquor (color)

aroma	liquor (taste)

aroma check list

☐ bitter ☐ robust ☐ nutty ☐ earthy ☐ citrus ☐ flowery ☐ sweet ☐ delicate ☐ malty

☐ spciy ☐ woodsy ☐ smokey ☐ other _____

prepared with

☐ sugar ☐ milk ☐ cream ☐ lemon ☐ honey ☐ other _____

notes

is this tea good iced?	where this tea was purchased
☐ yes ☐ no	

would you buy again?	ideal for	rating
☐ yes ☐ no		☆☆☆☆☆

tea tasting notes

date	tea (name/brand/seller)	
country of orgin:		price

tea type

☐ black ☐ green ☐ white ☐ herbal ☐ oolong ☐ pu-erh ☐ fruit ☐ other

brewing method	dry leaves (amount)	water temp.	steeping time(s)

tea leaves	liquor (color)
aroma	liquor (taste)

aroma check list

☐ bitter ☐ robust ☐ nutty ☐ earthy ☐ citrus ☐ flowery ☐ sweet ☐ delicate ☐ malty

☐ spicy ☐ woodsy ☐ smokey ☐ other

prepared with

☐ sugar ☐ milk ☐ cream ☐ lemon ☐ honey ☐ other

notes

is this tea good iced?	where this tea was purchased	
☐ yes ☐ no		
would you buy again?	ideal for	rating
☐ yes ☐ no		☆☆☆☆☆

tea tasting notes

date	tea (name/brand/seller)		
country of orgin:			price

tea type

☐ black ☐ green ☐ white ☐ herbal ☐ oolong ☐ pu-erh ☐ fruit ☐ other _____

brewing method	dry leaves (amount)	water temp.	steeping time(s)

tea leaves	liquor (color)
aroma	liquor (taste)

aroma check list

☐ bitter ☐ robust ☐ nutty ☐ earthy ☐ citrus ☐ flowery ☐ sweet ☐ delicate ☐ malty

☐ spicy ☐ woodsy ☐ smokey ☐ other _____

prepared with

☐ sugar ☐ milk ☐ cream ☐ lemon ☐ honey ☐ other _____

notes

is this tea good iced?	where this tea was purchased	
☐ yes ☐ no		
would you buy again?	ideal for	rating
☐ yes ☐ no		☆ ☆ ☆ ☆ ☆

tea tasting notes

date	tea (name/brand/seller)

country of orgin:	price

tea type

☐ black ☐ green ☐ white ☐ herbal ☐ oolong ☐ puerh ☐ fruit ☐ other _____

brewing method	dry leaves (amount)	water temp.	steeping time(s)

tea leaves	liquor (color)

aroma	liquor (taste)

aroma check list

☐ bitter ☐ robust ☐ nutty ☐ earthy ☐ citrus ☐ flowery ☐ sweet ☐ delicate ☐ malty

☐ spicy ☐ woodsy ☐ smokey ☐ other _____

prepared with

☐ sugar ☐ milk ☐ cream ☐ lemon ☐ honey ☐ other _____

notes

is this tea good iced?	where this tea was purchased
☐ yes ☐ no	

would you buy again?	ideal for	rating
☐ yes ☐ no		☆ ☆ ☆ ☆ ☆

tea tasting notes

date	tea (name/brand/seller)

country of orgin:		price

tea type

☐ black ☐ green ☐ white ☐ herbal ☐ oolong ☐ pu-erh ☐ fruit ☐ other _____

brewing method	dry leaves (amount)	water temp.	steeping time(s)

tea leaves	liquor (color)

aroma	liquor (taste)

aroma check list

☐ bitter ☐ robust ☐ nutty ☐ earthy ☐ citrus ☐ flowery ☐ sweet ☐ delicate ☐ malty

☐ spicy ☐ woodsy ☐ smokey ☐ other _____

prepared with

☐ sugar ☐ milk ☐ cream ☐ lemon ☐ honey ☐ other _____

notes

is this tea good iced?	where this tea was purchased	
☐ yes ☐ no		

would you buy again?	ideal for	rating
☐ yes ☐ no		☆☆☆☆☆

tea tasting notes

date	tea (name/brand/seller)	
country of orgin:		price

tea type

☐ black   ☐ green   ☐ white   ☐ herbal   ☐ oolong   ☐ pu-erh   ☐ fruit   ☐ other _____

brewing method	dry leaves (amount)	water temp.	steeping time(s)

tea leaves	liquor (color)
aroma	liquor (taste)

aroma check list

☐ bitter   ☐ robust   ☐ nutty   ☐ earthy   ☐ citrus   ☐ flowery   ☐ sweet   ☐ delicate   ☐ malty

☐ spciy   ☐ woodsy   ☐ smokey   ☐ other _____

prepared with

☐ sugar   ☐ milk   ☐ cream   ☐ lemon   ☐ honey   ☐ other _____

notes

is this tea good iced?	where this tea was purchased	
☐ yes ☐ no		
would you buy again?	ideal for	rating
☐ yes ☐ no		☆ ☆ ☆ ☆ ☆

tea tasting notes

date	tea (name/brand/seller)		
country of orgin:			price

tea type

☐ black ☐ green ☐ white ☐ herbal ☐ oolong ☐ puerh ☐ fruit ☐ other _____

brewing method	dry leaves (amount)	water temp.	steeping time(s)
tea leaves		liquor (color)	
aroma		liquor (taste)	

aroma check list

☐ bitter ☐ robust ☐ nutty ☐ earthy ☐ citrus ☐ flowery ☐ sweet ☐ delicate ☐ malty
☐ spicy ☐ woodsy ☐ smokey ☐ other _____

prepared with

☐ sugar ☐ milk ☐ cream ☐ lemon ☐ honey ☐ other _____

notes

is this tea good iced? ☐ yes ☐ no	where this tea was purchased	
would you buy again? ☐ yes ☐ no	ideal for	rating ☆☆☆☆☆

tea tasting notes

date	tea (name/brand/seller)

country of orgin:	price

tea type

☐ black   ☐ green   ☐ white   ☐ herbal   ☐ oolong   ☐ puerh   ☐ fruit   ☐ other _____

brewing method	dry leaves (amount)	water temp.	steeping time(s)

tea leaves	liquor (color)

aroma	liquor (taste)

aroma check list

☐ bitter   ☐ robust   ☐ nutty   ☐ earthy   ☐ citrus   ☐ flowery   ☐ sweet   ☐ delicate   ☐ malty

☐ spciy   ☐ woodsy   ☐ smokey   ☐ other _____

prepared with

☐ sugar   ☐ milk   ☐ cream   ☐ lemon   ☐ honey   ☐ other _____

notes

is this tea good iced?	where this tea was purchased
☐ yes ☐ no	

would you buy again?	ideal for	rating
☐ yes ☐ no		☆ ☆ ☆ ☆ ☆

tea tasting notes

date	tea (name/brand/seller)	
country of orgin:		price

tea type

☐ black ☐ green ☐ white ☐ herbal ☐ oolong ☐ pu-erh ☐ fruit ☐ other _____

brewing method	dry leaves (amount)	water temp.	steeping time(s)

tea leaves	liquor (color)

aroma	liquor (taste)

aroma check list

☐ bitter ☐ robust ☐ nutty ☐ earthy ☐ citrus ☐ flowery ☐ sweet ☐ delicate ☐ malty
☐ spciy ☐ woodsy ☐ smokey ☐ other _____

prepared with

☐ sugar ☐ milk ☐ cream ☐ lemon ☐ honey ☐ other _____

notes

is this tea good iced?	where this tea was purchased	
☐ yes ☐ no		
would you buy again?	ideal for	rating
☐ yes ☐ no		☆☆☆☆☆

tea tasting notes

date	tea (name/brand/seller)

country of orgin:	price

tea type

☐ black ☐ green ☐ white ☐ herbal ☐ oolong ☐ pu-erh ☐ fruit ☐ other _____

brewing method	dry leaves (amount)	water temp.	steeping time(s)

tea leaves	liquor (color)

aroma	liquor (taste)

aroma check list

☐ bitter ☐ robust ☐ nutty ☐ earthy ☐ citrus ☐ flowery ☐ sweet ☐ delicate ☐ malty

☐ spicy ☐ woodsy ☐ smokey ☐ other _____

prepared with

☐ sugar ☐ milk ☐ cream ☐ lemon ☐ honey ☐ other _____

notes

is this tea good iced? ☐ yes ☐ no	where this tea was purchased

would you buy again? ☐ yes ☐ no	ideal for	rating ☆☆☆☆☆

www.ingramcontent.com/pod-product-compliance
Lightning Source LLC
Chambersburg PA
CBHW071408080526
44587CB00017B/3211